The Tree and the Sun

By Heather Reilly

© 2000 by Heather Cousins
© 2013 by Heather Reilly
All rights reserved. The book's author retains sole copyright to all intellectual contributions to this book, including but not limited to text and images.

No part of this publication may be reproduced, stored in a retrieval system, or transmitted in any form or by any means, electronic, mechanical, photocopying, recording, or otherwise, without written permission from the author.

ISBN: **978-0-9919367-5-5**

This book is dedicated to the readers of bedtime stories.

It is also for Evelyn Black and Pat Lychek.
Thank you for having faith in me,
and for giving me a chance.

Once long ago in a village by the water, there lived a boy and girl. The boy, Raymond, was sturdy and strong with brown eyes, black hair, and a love for music. The girl, Flora, was quick and beautiful with green eyes, red hair, and a love for dance. Sometimes, they would go into the forest where no one could hear, and he would play for her songs on his penny whistle and she would dance around him to the melodic sound of his music.

Although they were allowed to go into the forest, their parents would warn them of a lake at the end of the path. "Now mind that you don't go into the water!" their parents would say. "Legend has it that the lake is enchanted, and anyone who so much as sets foot in it will instantly turn to water, becoming part of the lake itself."

Raymond and Flora grew up together, were best friends in fact, and they loved each other dearly. Every day they would play their imaginative games; they would roar and pretend to be beasts, or they would be heroes and would chase away imaginary villains.

They loved their games and time together, and as they grew, they fell in love. Raymond would often become inspired and would write poetry or songs for Flora, and she in turn would write letters or sketch pictures for Raymond in their time apart.

While in each other's company, they still played their games, but now they were more intimate games of chase that often took them through the village and into the forest that surrounded it and the lake. Inevitably, one day, Fauna caught Raymond and tripped, and they went spilling down the leafy slope to the beautiful sandy beach.

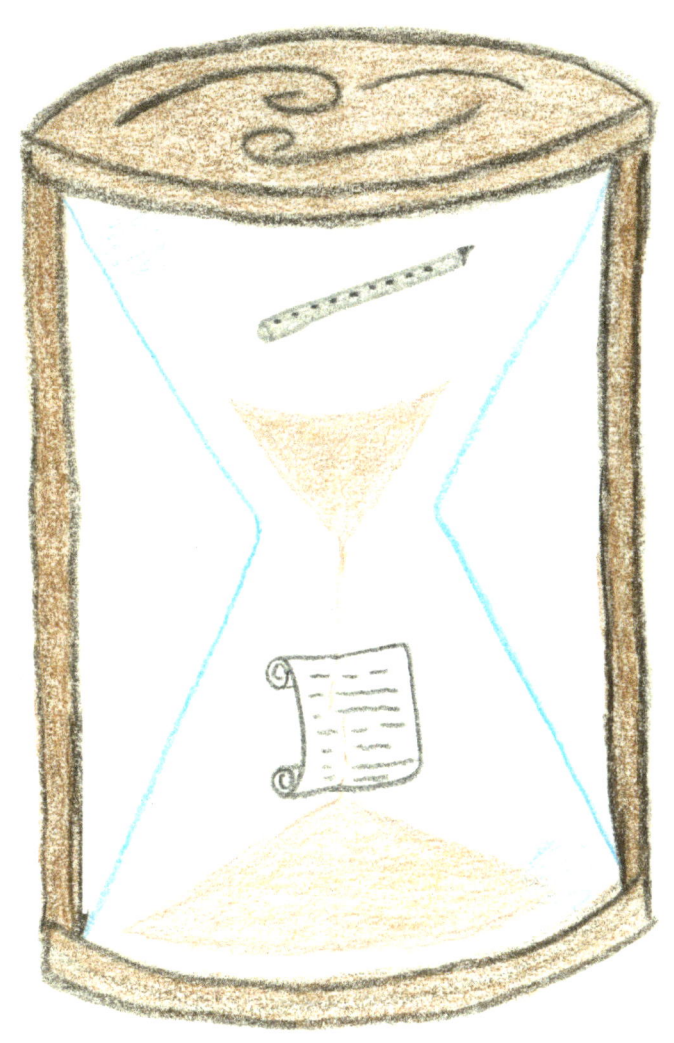

Curious, and a little too old to believe the stories of his childhood, Raymond drew near to the waves lapping up onto the shore and peered into the clear water. "Raymond, no!" Flora warned, "It isn't safe!" Raymond stepped away, but his interest was now awakened.

Raymond stayed away from the beach for a week, but then his inquisitiveness got the better of him. He just had to go back and get another look. He explained to Flora that they were older now, and the beach was a perfectly safe place. But Flora trusted her parents, and believed them when they said the water was dangerous. She refused to go. He asked, then begged, then pleaded with her to go with him. She finally agreed, upon his promise that they would stay away from the water's edge.

One day, Raymond and Flora packed a picnic lunch and prepared to go for a walk on the beach in the dreamy sunshine. As they were strolling slowly through the forest, Raymond turned to Flora with a mischievous glint in his eye. "I have a surprise for you!" he said. "Oh, what is it?" she asked, excited.   "You'll just have to wait, until we reach the water's edge," he replied, glad to see her amusement. They skipped hand in hand while Raymond carried the basket, down the slope to the sandy beach.

There, laying half in the sand and half in the gently lapping water was a glorious little wooden rowboat. Flora clapped her hands and jumped in delight.

"Surprise!" Raymond said, very happy that she was so taken with his idea. "Now we can go out on the water without having to touch it! He explained with a wink.

Flora immediately climbed into the boat and Raymond handed her the picnic basket. She set it down and Raymond pushed the boat off the shore, being careful not to get his feet wet, before climbing into the boat himself. They weren't in the boat long, before clouds shaded the bright sun. The couple was so entranced with the fish under the surface of the water, that they didn't notice the weather change at all. The dark clouds began to thunder and rumble, opening up to drench the young couple in a cold downpour.

The little wooden boat started getting tossed about on the mounting waves, and they grasped the sides of the boat to keep from going overboard. The picnic basket got thrown into the water. There was a loud *SPLOOSH*, then nothing...no sign of the picnic basket at all. Raymond and Flora looked over the side of the boat in amazement, realizing that the old wives' tale was true.

Another huge wave hit them and almost spilled into the boat. Flora lost her grip on the gunwales and pitched into the water, calling to Raymond for help. Raymond moved quickly to catch Flora's hand, but too late, and throwing the boat off balance with his movement, he tipped into the water after her.

As soon as they were submerged under the water, they felt weightless as they began to change. Looking down, all they saw was water. No hands, feet, bodies or heads. They were now just a part of the water itself. The water that was Flora and the water that was Raymond swirled together and felt complete.

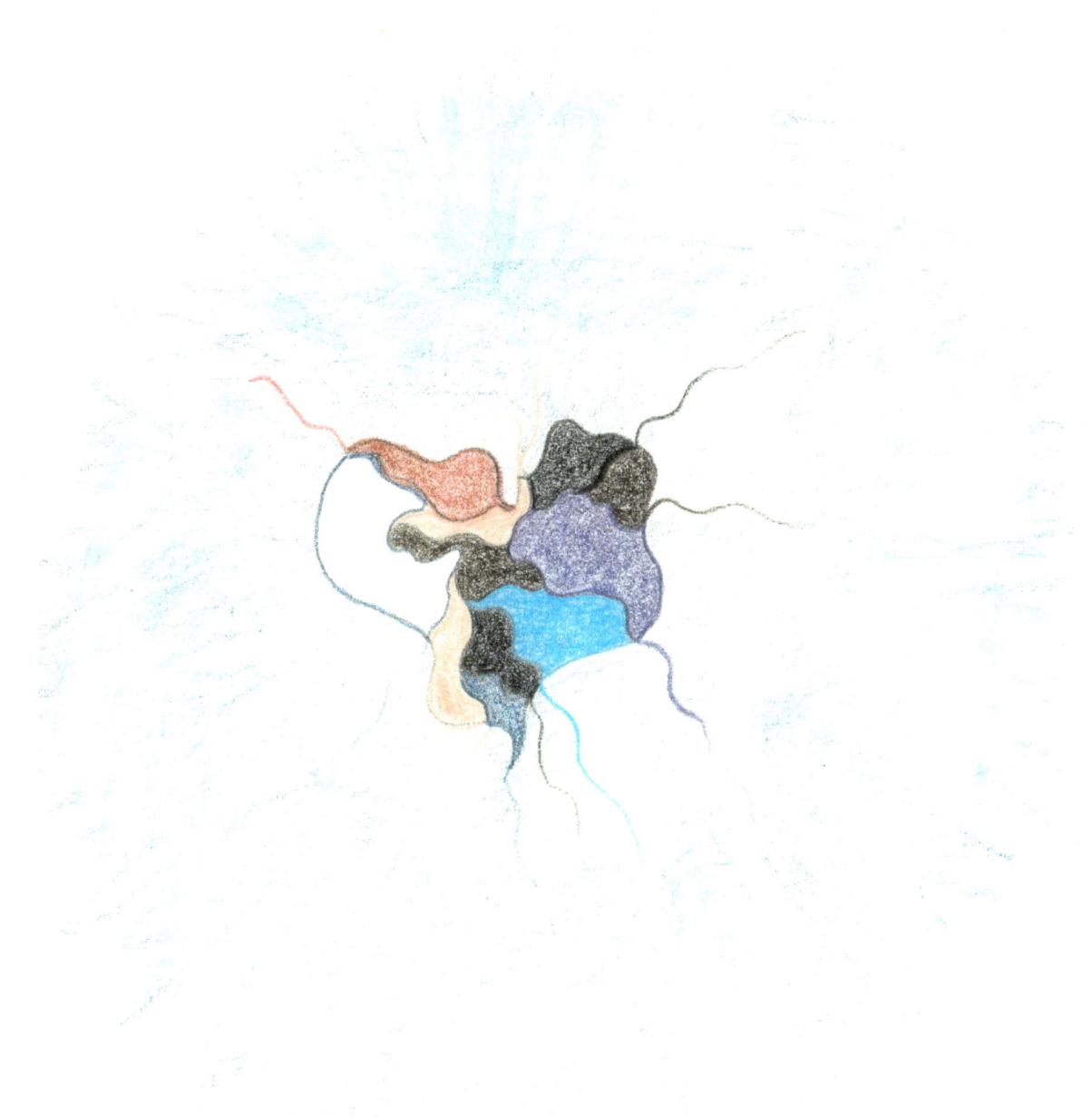

Eventually, the water that was Raymond evaporated and rose into the air, becoming a part of the sun. Now he was alone and sad, longing to be with Flora once again. Caught in the same feeling of misery, the water that was Flora allowed herself to be washed up on shore. She was soaked up by the roots of the forest and became part of a tree herself. Raymond saw this from his warm place in the sky and he shined down on Flora, reaching out to her with his sunny rays to touch her green leaves. Flora, in turn, lifted up her full branches to reach his warmth, so she was covered in his light, which helped her grow. That is how they stayed: Sun beaming down to tree, whose branches reached up to Sun, still in love's embrace, ever after.

Tree and Sun Experiment

This is a fun and interesting activity you can do in your class, or at home. It is great for the environment, and easier than you think to watch your very own plant or tree grow towards the Sun. You might even like to make it a special experiment for Earth Day in April.

This is how you give your plant everything it needs: **water**, **sun**, **earth**, and **air**.

Things you will need:
- Ziploc sandwich bag
- Paper towel
- Kidney Bean (your seed)
- Water
- Tape
- Window
- Small plant pot (approx. one week later)
- Potting soil (approx. one week later)

Step 1: Start with an empty, clean Ziploc sandwich bag.

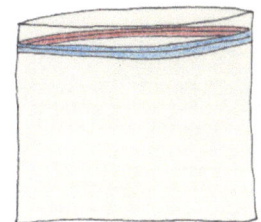

Step 2: Fold your paper towel into a rectangle small enough to easily fit into the bag. Get it wet, and place it in the bag.

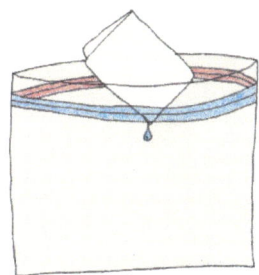

Step 3: Place the kidney bean in the bag against the paper towel. The water from the paper towel will feed the seed. Close the bag, and tape it to a window. The bean should be between the paper towel and the glass.

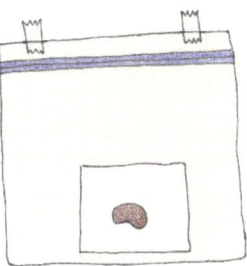

Check back each day to see how your seed starts to grow. If your paper towel starts to dry out, re-wet it, and check that your bag is closed.

Over the next week to ten days, it will look something like this:

The *hypocotyl* **s**tarts to poke out of the bean, (it looks like a little tail). This will become the part of the plant between the *roots* and the *leaves*.

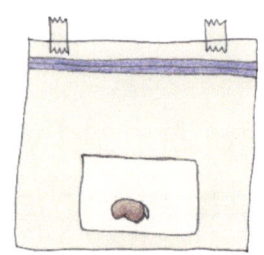

Your plant will continue to grow, and the *seed coat* will start to loosen as the *cotyledons* start to emerge. (They look almost like a little bean themselves).

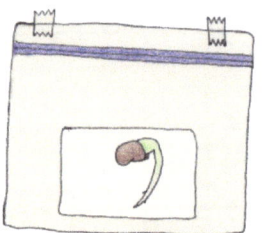

Roots will form, the *seed coat* will fall free of the plant, and your first *leaves* will form.

Note: lots of things can affect how quickly your seed grows, so don't get discouraged if it's taking longer than expected. Everything from room and water temperatures, to amount of sunlight can all play a factor. Some seeds never grow, so try this experiment with more than one bag, just in case.

Now you are ready to move your bean plant to the soil!

Fill your plant pot almost to the top with soil. (You want the soil to be loose, not packed in like brown sugar).

Use your finger to bore down into the center of the soil to make a hole that your plant will go in. The hole should be deep enough that all of your roots will be covered. It should be wide enough that you can put your plant's roots safely into the hole without breaking them off.

Once your roots are in the hole, add more soil to fill the remaining space. Gently press down the top of the soil around your plant to make sure it is secure.

Water your plant to keep the soil moist, keep it in sunlight, and see what happens. Take a photo each day to make a scrap book of its growth when the experiment is over. See if you can answer these questions over the next couple of weeks:

- *How many centimeters or inches does it grow each day?*
- *How many days pass between each stage of growth?*
- *Does the whole bean plant grow towards the sun?*
- *Do the leaves turn toward the sun/window?*
- *Do the leaves droop or rise when you water your plant?*

Note: there are two variations you can do for this experiment:

1) You can skip the whole baggie process and start with the soil in the pot. To do this, you fill the pot with soil, make sure the soil is very wet all the time, and just lay the beans on top (I would recommend 1-6 beans per pot). Observe and keep the soil wet over the next two weeks. As the bean plants emerge, they will plant themselves!

2) Use maple keys (or "helicopters", as kids like to call them), to grow your own maple tree! You need to go outside and collect the keys when they are still green and soft. Fill your pot with soil, and lay the keys on top as with the beans in the step above.

Interesting plant facts:

Some plants allow their leaves to droop outside on a hot day to conserve moisture. Others, like those with large flat leaves, (like tomatoes or black-eyed-susans,) don't conserve moisture, so if their leaves are drooping, it means there might not be enough moisture in their root system and they are beginning to wilt.

Which type do you think your bean plants are?

The leaves or stems of many plants will seem to turn toward the sun as they grow.

This process is called *positive phototropism,* and is a result of a plant hormone called *auxin* in the side of the plant farthest from the light. The cells there become elongated, making the plant grow unevenly. This allows the leaves to soak up the most amount of light to allow for *photosynthesis* , the plant's process of using sunlight to generate energy.

Azuki bean plants will bend towards the light. Do you think your kidney bean plants will do the same thing, or do you think they will act differently because they are a different type of bean?

The leaves of the aloe vera plant, (that look like tentacles,) can show a great example of *positive phototropism*. If the plant is indoors, it will grow toward the window. If you turn the plant pot, the leaves will start to grow the other way, always toward the sunlight.

Other books by Heather Reilly:

YA Novels:

Binding of the Almatraek
Book I: *Knight's Surrender*

Binding of the Almatraek
Book II: *Noble Pursuit*

Children's:

*Tock-Tick-Tock,
The Mouse and the Clock*

Upcoming Novels:

Binding of the Almatraek
Book III: *Enchanted Page*

Learn more about the author and her books at:
www.reillybooks.com

Titles are also available at amazon.com,
and on ebook at smashwords.com

www.ingramcontent.com/pod-product-compliance
Lightning Source LLC
Chambersburg PA
CBHW060800090426
42736CB00002B/97